100

New Zealand Poems

for Children

This Book belongs to...

ISAAC
PATTISON

:)

100
New Zealand Poems
for Children

Edited by **Jo Noble**

Illustrations by **David Elliot**

RANDOM HOUSE
NEW ZEALAND

A RANDOM HOUSE BOOK
Published by
Random House New Zealand
18 Poland Road, Glenfield, Auckland, New Zealand

First published 1999, reprinted 1999, 2000, 2001

© 1999 Selection and foreword: Jo Noble; poems: as credited on p. 8;
illustrations: David Elliot

ISBN 1 86941 404 7

Design: Christine Hansen
Cover illustration: David Elliot
Printed in Hong Kong

Contents

6

Foreword

How do you write a poem?

Do you feel it coming on, like a cold or a headache? Do you then have to sit down and work on it, word by word, until you know it's just right? Or is the idea suddenly there, in your head, all ready to be written down? Then maybe you have to spend that time thinking about the words, making sure they say just what you want.

The poems in this book have come out of the heads of all sorts of different people and we have not tried to sort them out into any special order. It's a book to be dipped into and browsed through, and enjoyed by anyone at any time.

There are poems here that will make you laugh, some that may make you want to cry; there are short poems and long poems, poems that tell a story and poems that make a picture for you inside your head.

The only thing they have in common is that they are all New Zealand poems. Some of them are by poets who are no longer living but whose poetry has become part of our culture, but most are by poets still living, many of them by people whose names you know well, like Margaret Mahy and Joy Cowley, Alan Bagnall and Peggy Dunstan.

And some of them are by children, which is an extra–special joy. They're not chosen because they're the best poems by children we could find, but were chosen at random out of the many hundreds that children keep writing at home and at school.

We hope you will enjoy this book and that it will nudge many more young people into writing their poetry down and not leaving it locked up inside their heads.

Jo Noble, July 1999

Acknowledgements

The publishers gratefully acknowledge the following authors, publishers, literary agencies and copyright holders for permission to reproduce the numbered poems. LML = Learning Media Ltd, AS = Ashton Scholastic. 1: © Judy Ling, 1997 (LML); 2, 3: © Pauline Cartwright, 1997, (LML); 4: © Pauline Cartwright, 1996, (LML); 5, 6: © Laura Ranger, 1995 Godwit; 7: © Sam Young, 1999; 8: © Tui Boyle; 9: © Elliot Smith, 1999; 10: © Alan Bagnall, 1996, (LML); 11: © Riley Dunn, 1996 (LML); 12: © Rachel McAlpine, 1996 (LML); 13: © Alan Bagnall, 1995, (LML); 14: © Jane Buxton, 1995, (LML); 15: © Stuart Payne, 1990 (LML); 16: © Eileen Duggan; 17: © Don Franks, 1994 (LML); 18, 37, 55, 63, 66, 67, 93, 97: © Peggy Dunstan; 19: © Bev Kemp, 1992 (LML); 20: © Attributed to J.A. Tole, rediscovered by Gwenyth Jones; 21: © Gwenyth Jones, 1990 (LML); 22: © Anne R. McDonell, 1985 (LML); 23: © Fiona Farrell, 1994; 24: © Alan Bagnall, 1990, (LML); 25, 26, 65: © Alan Trussell-Cullen, 1992, (AS); 27, 95: © Joy Watson, 1992 (AS); 28, 94, 87: © The Estate of Denis Glover, Granville Glover Family Trust; 29: © Joy Cowley, Richards Literary Agency; 30: © Ron Bacon; 31: © Harry Ellwood*, 1992 (AS); 32: © Ruth Dallas, The Caxton Press; 33: © E. Muriel Attewell, Whitcombe and Tombs Ltd; 34: © Allen Curnow, Oxford University Press; 35: © Alistair Te Ariki Campbell, Pegasus Press; 36, 82, 91: © Margaret Mahy, Orion Children's Books; 38: © Gwenyth Jones; 39, 96, 69, 71: © The Estate of James K. Baxter, Oxford University Press, Mrs J. Baxter; 40: © Elizabeth Taille, 1999 (LML); 41: © Diana Noonan, 1997 (LML); 42: © Jo Bowler, 1998 (LML); 43, 53: © Shirley Gawith, Treehouse; 44: © Jane Buxton, 1997 (LML); 45: © Shelley Peters, 1997 (LML); 46: © Jane Buxton, 1998 (LML); 47: © Ruby Corbet, 1998 (LML); 48, 50 © Lynn Frances, 1997 (LML); 49: © Belle Avery, 1989*; 51: © David Hill, 1994 (LML); 52: © Vivienne Joseph, 1995 (LML); 54: © Susan Devereux, 1992 (LML); 56: © K. E. Anderson, 1996 (LML); 57: © Alwyn Owen, 1995 (LML); 58, 90: © Alan Bagnall, 1997, (LML); 59: © Roger Telenius, 1995 (LML); 60: © Nick Fenwick, 1988*; 61: © Peter Bland, 1984 (LML); 62: © Anne Adams, 1994 (LML); 64: © Elaine Lindsay, 1991*; 68, 88 © Shelwyn Lee, 1992 (AS); 70: © Ruth Corrin; 72: © Marlene Bennetts, 1991; 73: © Vivienne Joseph, 1996 (LML); 74: © April Wood, 1993*; 75: © Elizabeth Spencer, 1984*; 76: © Marion Rego, 1992 (LML); 77: © Tho En, 1993 (LML); 78: Text © Beth Braddock, 1992 (LML); 79: © Stuart Payne, 1992 (LML); 80: © Bernard Gadd, 1993 (LML); 81, 84, 89: © Jon Gadsby, 1995, Random House; 83: © Peter Bland; 85: © Rae A. Williams*; 86: © Howard Small*, 1992 (AS); 92: © Katherine Mansfield Estate, Constable and Company Ltd (Society of Authors as literary representative of the estate of Katherine Mansfield); 98: © Anon, 1991; 99: © Robert Laws (Estate), 1990*; 100: © Anna Beeson, 1999.
* Every endeavour was made to contact these authors but without success.

Dinosaur

—Judy Ling

Tyrannosaurus
Lived before us.
Ultrasaur
Is no more.
Pteranodon
Has been and gone.
Triceratops
Were awful flops.
And as for archaeopteryx,
They ended up in quite a fix.

9

2

The same old mum
—Pauline Cartwright

When Mum comes home from work,
the first thing she says is
'Put on the coffee, love,
I'll just go and change into something else.'

I put on the coffee and wait.
Will she change into a camel?
or a smiley green dragon?
or a chest of drawers?
or a triple-headed alien?
or maybe a super-mum
who cries 'Gazoo! Gazam!'

No, she always comes back the same old mum.
All she ever changes into
are her old home clothes.

3   Table manners
—Pauline Cartwright

When my uncle comes to tea,
I hate him sitting opposite me.
His mouth, when he eats, is open wide,
and it's AWFUL seeing straight inside
as the meat and vegies all go round
they make a sort of sloshing sound.

My mother should be very glad
my table manners aren't that bad.

4 So mad

—Pauline Cartwright

I'm so mad
that I'm never coming out of my room again!
Never ever, ever, EVER.
I'm so mad
that all of me, even my teeth, feels like red flames
burning, burning, burning!
I'm so mad
that I could shrivel anyone with a single look,
a glaring, staring look!
I'm so mad
that I could push the walls of our house right over!
Crash! Bash! Smash!
I'm so mad
that I'm never coming out of my room again!
Never. Ever. Ever. EVER.

Well, not until teatime, anyway.

Tulip Sunday

—Laura Ranger (6)

In the Botanical Gardens
bright tulips
spread out
like a yellow tablecloth
on a table with thousands of legs.

Some tulips
have red lips
and dark black eyes.
They bow and curtsy
in the wind.

Disappear
—Laura Ranger (8)

Boys are annoying.
I am going to send
my little brother
to the furthest planet
away from earth.
My disappearing spell
is a gross mixture
of frog's blood and pearls
to give him warts.
I will send spies to
see if it has worked.
I have a secret word
but I cannot tell.
The hardest part
of the spell
is getting him
to drink it.

Riding for defeat

—Sam Young (10)
of Tikipunga School, Whangarei

Hop on my bike.
Down the hill.
Too fast.
Cannot see.
Smash in the tree.
Dead old me.
Poor dead me.
No helmet you see.

8 Like a bird in a cage
—Tui Boyle (11)
of Amworth School, Papakura

Like a bird in a cage
Got nowhere to fly,
Nothing to do
Just sit there and cry.

Like a prisoner in his cell
Just sits there and waits,
Hoping that someone
Will open the gates.

Nothing to do
Not a thing.
Feeling quite sad
And got no song to sing.

Looking outside
It's a bright sunny day.
The door has been open
So I can fly away.

9 Play on words

—Elliott Smith (8) of Christchurch

My funny bone's not funny
my eye teeth cannot see.

You don't hammer fingernails
shoulder blades don't cut me.

Jawbones aren't eaten by dogs
eardrums aren't in bands. We

don't wear belly buttons on
shirts or tie el-bows. Be

warned that my knees don't wear caps
this play on words—oh gee!

10

Food chain
—Alan Bagnall

From the sea shore
To the depths
Below the Continental Shelf,
Everybody goes
About their business
Eating everybody else.

My sort of bike

—Riley Dunn

(Std 2) of Onerahi Primary School

It's a panther, big and black,
With fire bursting out the back,
Sort of bike.

It's a shimmering and shiny,
Smooth but whiny
Sort of bike.

Hooning down the highway
Late at night.
That's my sort of bike.

12

Skin-diving

—Rachel McAlpine

I sink below
this shiny blue skin
and I see the water
winking.

Help!
Kelp!
Straps
of vegetable leather
slap and shove
and hassle
the rocks and me—
I'm in a submarine
car-wash.

13 | Hesitation

—Alan Bagnall

I clasp my arms
About me, tight.
Shall I dive in?
I might, I might, I might.

Up to my middle
In the freezing river,
Others splash and squeal—
I just shiver, shiver, shiver.

14 | Smells

—Jane Buxton

I love . . .
The smell of the rain on the warm footpath,
the smell of our baby all clean from her bath,
the smell of clean sheets when Mum makes
   my bed,
and the smell in the kitchen when Dad's
  making bread.

I love . . .
the smell of the sea, all sharp, fresh and briny,
the smell of our Christmas tree, pungent and piny,
the smell of sweet peas climbing over the wall.
But the warm smell of horses I love best of all . . .

A band of showers
—Stuart Payne

15

A Band of Showers will sweep the land
according to the weatherman.

All year long these devilish hordes
scourge our towns on a front so broad
ravaging down across the plain
phalanx of sleet, attendant rain.

A Band of Showers
galloping ride
A Band of Showers
Threatening stride

Silver jewelled in a smoky gray
scattering all in disarray
swirled about in their capes of mist
rapping the roofs with flailing fists.

A Band of Showers
threatening stride
A Band of Showers
galloping ride.

So beware, take care, stay out of the way
when A Band of Showers strikes later today.

16 The song of the kingfisher
—Eileen Duggan

Why do you sit, so dreamily dreamily,
Kingfisher over the stream
Silent your beak, and silent the water,
What is your dream?

A falling, a flashing of blue and of silver,
Child, he is deep in the stream,
Prey in his beak and fear in the water
That was his dream!

17 My other jandal
—Don Franks

Have you seen my other jandal?
I had it just before.
It shouldn't be too hard to find—
it's somewhere on the shore.
It disappeared all by itself
when I was in the waves,
and that's the way my other jandal
usually behaves.

Have you seen my other jandal?
It's green with white on top.
It's still quite newish looking,
'cause it's just come from the shop.
I need my other jandal—
the sand's too hot to touch.
If you found my jandal for me
I'd thank you awfully much.

Have you seen my other jandal?
Mum says, 'Not *again*!
I'm sick of buying jandals—
Have a good look, use your brain!
Did you leave it in the dairy
when we went to get a drink?
Or is it down beside the rockpool?
Look, it must be somewhere. *Think*!'

Have you seen my other jandal?
It isn't in the car.
Without a foot to walk in it,
It can't have gone too far.
I wish that I could stop this—
It's been going on for years.
When summer starts,
my other jandal
always disappears.

Night countdown
—Peggy Dunstan

There are millions of stars
in the sky tonight
and thousands of lights on the hill.
There are hundreds of moths
round the thousands of lights
while the air is shining and still.
There are scores of noises
that music the night
and dozens of waves on the sea,
there's a chorus of barking,
a handful of squawks
but
only one moon
and one me.

19

Washday for the clouds
—Bev Kemp

The sky is drying
his shape-changing sheets
on the west wind today.

He rinsed the sheets
last night, and pounded them
on the thunder stones.

Tomorrow, when the sheets
have aired,
there will be dragons
and castles in the sky.

Oh how shall I cross the swift river

—Attributed to J.A. Tole

Ohau shall I cross the swift river Ohau?
Waikanae not swim to your shore?
Otaki a boat now and steadily row
In the Manawatu did before.
Oroua way gently, for life in a boat
Is a Horowhenua afloat.

Four cats
—Gwenyth Jones

21

Four cats owned a garden:
Rufus, Nimblefoot, Tibbles and Tommo.
And they planted—eyebright, speedwell,
milkweed, catmint, mouse ear, canary grass
Around the pussy willow.

Four cats roamed the garden:
Rufus, Nimblefoot, Tibbles and Tommo.
And they played at—tipcat, leapfrog,
four square, bullrush, hopscotch, hide and seek
Around the pussy willow.

Four cats praised their garden:
Rufus, Nimblefoot, Tibbles and Tommo.
And they chanted—humding, singsong,
purr-ur, meow-ow, scritch scratch, caterwaul
Around the pussy willow.

22

Sea witches
—Anne R. McDonell

Sea witches shampooed their hair today.
Bubbles lie piled on pools,
huge heaps of foam and froth
for the sea breezes to whisk away.
'Clean hair. Clean hair,' do we hear them say?
Their raucous cackling
their wicked wily laughter
sailing seawards on the salty spray.

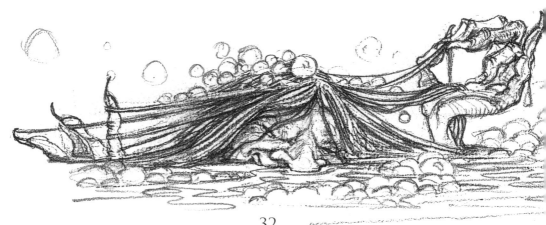

23 Underneath

—Fiona Farrell

Have you ever been walking and wondered
what exactly is under your feet?
First, the grass or pavement, nice
and neat. And under that, clay or river
stones worn smooth, or ash, or silt.
And then the rock. Miles of it with
canyons, caves and streams,
deep as forever and
dark as dreams.
And under that,
there's fire,
rock melted
at white
heat.

And that's
what's there
beneath
your
walking
feet.

Moods

—Alan Bagnall

I stumped off, angrily,
Far away from
My stupid family.

I think I even quite enjoyed
Kicking cow pats,
I was so annoyed.

By the open sea I sat for hours.
Then, wandering around,
I picked wild flowers—

A big bright bunch,
Carried home
In time for lunch.

Warning

—Alan Trussell-Cullen

Beware of the fly that
offers you a blow by blow
account of what he's
been doing.

Thinkery

26

—Alan Trussell-Cullen

For all the things I hear and see
I have this thing called a memory.
It holds on fast to what I wish,
To anything quite usefullish,
And everything else, regrettably,
Gets lost in my forgettory.

27 Alphabet stew
—Joy Watson

Apples and **B**rown bread, and **C**ream cheese on crackers;
Drumsticks and **E**ggnogs, and **F**ish fried in batter;
Grapefruit and **H**oney, and **I**ce-cream cake too—
these are all part of our alphabet stew.

Jelly and **K**iwifruit, **L**amb's fry and **M**ince
Nectarines, **O**ysters, **P**otatoes and **Q**uince;
Rhubarb and **S**ausage; **T**omatoes in sauce—
alphabet stew keeps us healthy of course!

Upside-down pudding, and **V**eal (thinly sliced);
Whitebait fritters, and **X**mas cake, iced;
Yams and **Z**ucchinis, to name just a few—
all mixed together make alphabet stew.

28 Drift

—Denis Glover

Drift drift upon the beach
Dead Man's Bay and Dead Man's Reach
Driftwood dunks and driftwood rides
Inert upon the endless tides
Debris down the river drifting
Debris of the ocean's sifting
Sullen log and sodden boot
Tangled in the mangrove root
Upturned boat and empty tin
Drifting out and drifting in
One storm took them one storm more
May drive them to the indifferent shore
Castaways of wind and weather
Drifting aimlessly together.

29

Muddly, muddly
—Joy Cowley

Muddly, muddly,
Feed a lizard.
Stuff an earwig
In its gizzard,
Cut its toenails
In a blizzard.
Muddly, muddly,
Feed a lizard.

Muddly, muddly,
Feed a spider.
Drop a dragonfly
Inside her,
Put her in your
Hair, and hide her.
Muddly, muddly
Feed a spider.

Muddly, muddly,
Feed a goat.
Shove a cabbage
Down his throat.
Sit him in a
Paper boat.
Muddly, muddly,
Feed a goat.

The wind woman
—Ron Bacon

30

There is a land where grey ghost trees grasp the ground
with crooked finger roots,
where winter's snows lie white and deep
and thunderclouds clump the skies.
And on the mountain where soft mists surge and blow,
there is a great rock, black and craggy.

But summer comes and rainbows rise
and flowers star the grasses.
Then the wind woman leaves the lands below
and climbs the mountain.
Quietly she comes in the dawn of the morning,
when birdtalk is sleepy and slow.

She sits by the rock in the grass and the flowers,
and she spreads her skirts wide.
And when the sun's bright eye is high over the mountain,
she tosses her head and she unties her hair so it falls
loose and free.
Then she combs it and she plaits it
and she braids it with a ribbon of sky.

She whets her knife on the rock to make it sharp and keen—
once for the east wind, once for the west,
once for the wind that blows down from the north,
and once for the wind that roars up from the south.
She stays by the rock till day's end is near
and evening's airs are chilled.

Then, as night fills the valleys
and creeps over all the lands around,

she leaves the mountain
and goes down to the forest below.

And when a thousand years have passed and gone,
the wind woman will return to the mountain
to sit by the rock, to toss her head and tie her hair tight.
She will whet her knife on the rock once, twice, three times
and four on the rock.

Then she will gather her skirts around her
and go down the mountain
to the forests and farms below.

And a thousand years on
the wind woman will come again—and again,
until ten times ten thousand years and more have passed.

She will toss her head and tie her hair,
and whet her knife
and then go down the mountain
to the forests and the farms and the cities below.

And each time she comes and whets her knife
a speck of rock no more than
the dust of a butterfly's wing
is worn away.

And time passes until a time comes when
the rock is worn to dust and sand.
Then the wind woman will call her winds to blow
and the rains to fall
so the sands will scatter
and the rock will be no more.

And when the rock is gone
and daisies grow where once it stood,
one day of Forever will have passed.
Then, by another rock, on another hill,
the wind woman will sit and toss her head
and untie her hair . . .

Cricket

—Harry Ellwood

31

On summer nights
When summer moths
Fly soft on powdered wings;
When summer moon
Sails through the stars,
Then the cricket sings.

A fly

—Ruth Dallas

32

If I could
See this fly
With unprejudiced eye,
I should see his body
Was metallic blue—no,
Peacock blue.
His wings are a frosty puff;
His legs fine wire.
He even has a face,
I notice.
And he breathes, as I do.

33

To the show
—E. Muriel Attewell

They tied a halter round my head,
They pushed me here and there,
They patted me and prodded me,
And taught me how to lead.
They brushed at me and scrubbed at me,
Then lathered me with soap,
They clipped my hair and frizzed my tail
And polished horns and hooves.
They took me in a jolting truck
Onto the showground gay,
Then washed and brushed and spruced some more
And fed me wisps of hay.
They led me round and round the ring
While knowing judges stared—
But I was not a champion,
And came home—just a cow!

34 Wild Iron

—Allen Curnow

Sea go dark, or dark with wind,
Feet go heavy, heavy with sand,
Thoughts go wild, wild with the sound
Of iron on the old shed swinging, clanging:
Go dark, go heavy, go wild, go round,
        Dark with the wind,
        Heavy with the sand,
Wild with the iron that tears at the nail
And the foundering shriek of the gale.

35

Haiku
—Alistair Campbell

Listlessly on bare bough
a cicada scrapes
with his bow a few dry notes.

36

The remarkable cake
—Margaret Mahy

It's Christmas—the time when we gather to make
A truly remarkable once-a-year cake.
The recipe's written in letters of gold
By a family witch who is terribly old.

The rule of this cake is it has to be made
In a wheelbarrow (stirred with a shovel or spade)
At Christmas, the season of love and goodwill.
Other times of the year it might make you feel ill.

You must nail it together or stick it with glue,
Then hammer it flat with the heel of your shoe.
You must stretch it out thin, you must tie it in knots,
Then get out your paint box and paint it with spots.

What a taste! What a flavour! It's certain to please
It's rather like ice cream with pickles and cheese.
In June it would taste like spaghetti and mud,
While its taste in September would curdle your blood.

Oh, what a cake! It looks simply delicious.
Now get out the carving knife, get out the dishes!
Be careful! Be careful! This cake might explode,
And blow up the kitchen and part of the road.

51

Oh dear! It's exploded! I thought that it might.
It's not very often we get it just right.
Let's comfort the baby, revive Uncle Dan,
And we'll start it all over as soon as we can.

For Christmas—that gypsy day—it comes
    and it goes
Far sooner than ever we dare to suppose.
Once more in December we'll gather to make
That truly remarkable once-a-year cake.

Still, I wouldn't like to be one

—Peggy Dunstan

A worm's life is a happy one
just sitting around
enjoying sun
without the need of any friend—
    conversing
with its other end.

Skipping rhyme

—Gwenyth Jones

Mane, Mane, one, two, three,
Turei, Turei, skip with me.
Wenerei, Wenerei, turn around,
Taite, Taite, touch the ground.
Paraire, Paraire, touch the sky,
Ra Horoi, rope swings high.
Ra Tapu, you're too slow—
End of the week, so out you go!
    (Pepper)

The gorse fire
—James K. Baxter

39

Oh what a worry
When the gorse bushes catch!
Somebody careless
Has dropped a match.

Somebody careless
Let it fall down,
Took no notice
That the grass was brown.

A little thin flame
Came galloping fast
Then roared up higher
Than the top of a mast.

The black smoke climbed
Like a tower in the sky
Till there was no room
For the birds to fly.

And the crackling bushes
Blazed higher and higher
Up the brown hillside
Like a river on fire!

Looking up, looking down
—Elizabeth Taillie

I lie on my back and look at the sky,
watching the clouds go racing by.
If I screw up my eyes, I can almost see
The leaves on top of the kowhai tree.
The row of pine trees over the wall
must be a hundred metres tall,
and everything makes me feel so small!

I lie on my tummy, very still,
and hardly move at all until
I see a movement in the grass
and watch a tiny spider pass.
Some ants are crawling over a twig,
a little beetle starts to dig—
and everything makes me feel so **BIG**!

Bugs, bugs, bugs

—Diana Noonan

There are bugs on our cauliflowers
there are bugs on our beans.
There are bugs on our tomatoes
and bugs on our greens.
There are bugs, bugs, bugs
on the peas and carrots too.
Our garden's not a garden—
our garden is a zoo!

42

Creatures
—Jo Bowler

There's a rhino in my bathtub.
There's a weta by my plate,
an iguana in my wardrobe
and a bison at my gate.

There's an ostrich in the kitchen
and a leopard in my bed.
There's a sloth up in the rafters
and a toucan on my head.

There's a little kiwi snoozing
on a cushion on the floor.
There's an elephant upon the couch
and more outside the door.

There's a lemur playing tennis
while the monkeys watch TV—
all the creatures in the world
can come and live with me.

The boa
—Shirley Gawith

I should think even Noah disliked the big boa,
For a boa comes slinking with never a sound,
Slithering, slithering, over the ground,
And around and around it will wrap you as neat
As a parcel for posting, from head down to feet.
Then without a polite 'may I?' or a 'please',
It will tighten its grip in a breath-taking squeeze.

43

44

Dinner play

—Jane Buxton

Mashed potato mountains
and broccoli trees,
A sea of brown gravy
And hills of green peas,
Diced carrot houses,
An island of meat—
Dinner is more fun
To play with than eat!

Sunflower
—Shelley Peters

45

Are you looking at me
with your one eye?
Can you see me when I go by?
As I watch you
sway and bend,
are you saying, 'Hello,
my friend'?

Socks

—Jane Buxton

Red socks and yellow socks,
purple socks and pink.
Clean socks and not-so-clean
and socks that really stink.

Striped socks and spotted socks
and socks with lace and bows.
Long socks and short socks
And socks with holey toes.

Socks! Socks! So many socks!
I've got socks to spare.
But, however hard I look,
I can never find a pair.

Sports report

—Ruby Corbet

Gordon Gore was never sporty
Till he reached the age of forty
When the *Weekly Sport* recorded
All the things that Gordon did—
Skiing, skating, jazzogenics,
Soccer, softball, callisthenics,
Tennis, baseball, rugby, rowing,
Wrestling, golf and javelin throwing,
Which explains at forty-five,
Why Gordon Gore is not alive.
We gather, now he's not about,
That Gordon—and his breath—ran out.

48

Seagulls

—Lynn Frances

Seagulls
perch on wire
tail feathers crossed
like fingers
behind them
for luck.

49 Skateboard

—Belle Avery

The old ladies trembled
when they saw me rolling
and rolling
speeding
and speeding
right from the top of the street.
They leaped to the side,
I think they stopped breathing
as I rumbled, clicket,
and I rumbled, clacket,
over the joints in the paving.
Louder
and louder,
nearer
and nearer,
faster
and faster,
with wind in my hair
and power in my thighs,
momentum
MOMENTUM!

The old ladies trembled
and rattled their wrinkles,
breathed in with a squeak
and out with a squawk,
their bright eyes boggled behind their bifocals
for in a red splotch by their long bony feet,
I motionless lay with the skin off my seat.

Rock bottom

—Lynn Frances

Would you believe it?
There's rock here.
Last week it was
covered by sand.

The sea in a temper
has swept that aside
and now I don't know
where I stand.

Don't be wet (a poem for two voices)
—David Hill

51

So you think you're a fish, Mr—
Fin.
And your favourite game is—
Pool.
A film that you hated was—
Hook.
And you met all your friends in a—
School.
Your father's a piano—
Tuna.
So each morning you check on your—
Scales.
The best book you've read was called—
Jaws.
You're expert at telling such—
Tails.
But say there's a bully called—
Rod.
And he's trodden quite hard on your—
'Eel.
That made you yell out a loud—
Whale.
Mr Fin, you believe this?
It's reel!

Palomino
—Vivienne Joseph

52

I like it when
        the wind climbs
sunburned hills
        and the grass shivers
like the hairs
        on a pony's back
and a toetoe mane
        flows over my shoulder
as we gallop
        and gallop
                and gallop away

53

The crocodile
—Shirley Gawith

A crocodile should never be
Asked in to share your Sunday tea.
He has no manners, is so rude
And greedy, he'd eat all the food.
And all the dishes too, and then
Before you counted up to ten,
You'd find he'd not just eaten most,
But also (probably) his host.

Day in spring
—Susan Devereux

54

Birds back in full cry,
Early morning, light sky.

Up at seven, nil breeze,
Shorts and sandals, bare knees.

Green shoots, budding flowers,
Pollen drifting, whizzing mowers.

Lunchtime showers, wind groans,
Grab a parka, hailstones.

Sixty knots, heavy seas,
Gales twisting stiff trees.

Blossom biffed about the path,
Just a moment! Storm's passed.

Sun's back, heat too,
Tonight we'll try the barbecue.

Daylight saving, cold but light,
What's next, frostbite?

It's difficult to get outside
And settle down to play
When the weather's throwing tantrums
Through the long spring day.

55 Today it snowed
—Peggy Dunstan

First hand
I do not know
very much
about snow.
But
there's a taste
a smell in the air
even before
it is there.
Light changes
and is faintly
silver,
strange.
And the wind blows.
Rain sleets and tumbles,
jumbles—
and it snows.

Time capsule
—K.E. Anderson

In a hundred years it'll be opened
By people you won't even know.
What will you put in your capsule?
What will you tell and show?

I'll take from the paper a clipping
That will tell of the Bosnian war.
I hope in one hundred years
They don't want to fight any more.

I'll write about nuclear weapons
The testing, the protests, the fear.
I'll warn the people next century
Earth needs tending and care.

I'll put in a picture of forests
And lakes and wide-open spaces.
In a hundred years from now
They may never have seen those places.

I'll put in a tape of music
Which I listen to every day.
I only hope in a hundred years
There are things on which it'll play.

In a hundred years it'll be opened
By people you won't even know,
What will you put in your capsule?
What will you tell and show?

The puma

—Alwyn Owen

57

No savage heart beats in the puma
It's really just a nasty rumour:
Indeed, the puma when he can
Will try to make a friend of Man,
And underneath his tawny hide
He's just a pussy-cat inside.
The puma's innermost desire
Is warm contentment by the fire,
Or curled up in a cosy chair.
Instead of these, he's forced to bear
The cold discomfort of his lair.

If you should want to keep a puma
Remember he's a big consumer:
He eats a lot, and chews his way
Through half a bullock every day.
So though he makes a cuddly pet,
You'll find it cheaper if you get
An animal not quite so big—
A rabbit, or a guinea pig.

58

My cat
—Alan Bagnall

My cat
becomes a tiger.
His eyes are
wide and bright.
He shimmers
in the shadows,
then melts
into the night.

Writing a poem

—Roger Telenius

59

When writing a poem
words turn up
like guests to a fancy-dress party;
old friends with new faces
who mingle and dance and
step on each other's toes and
shout and show off
or, who whisper shy secrets
that help in the search
for that last graceful phrase
that fits, sometimes,
like Cinderella's slipper.

Fiona's runny nose

—Nick Fenwick

Fiona's got a runny nose:
She wishes it would run away
To come again another day
And stick on someone ELSE'S head—
(That's what she said!)

She says she's god a ruddy doze
Because she's god a rodden code—
It's always wadding to be blode.
Because of it she's pud in bed—
(That's what she said!)

Fiona's got a runny nose.
She hasn't had to go to school.
But still she's feeling mizrabool,
It's made her hankenfitches wed—
(That's what she said!)

Fiona's got a runny nose.
'I see Fiona's little beak
Has got a most gig-ANTIC leak—
We'll have to plug it up with lead,'
Her father said.

But still her nose a-running goes:
She's tired of its silly pranks
And doesn't want much dinner, thanks,
For up she is completely fed—
(That's what she said!)

Owl

—Peter Bland

Night owl
　　　White owl
Cold stars
　　　Moon red
Attic light
　　　Fire bright
Earth sleep
　　　Warm bed.

61

62

Itches and snitches
—Anne Adams

Does anyone notice,
Or is it just me?
When everyone's quiet
As can possibly be,
Your nose always itches,
Your eyes start to run
You're dying to sneeze,
But it just doesn't come;
You make lots of noises,
And everyone stares;
You open your mouth—
Then the sneeze disappears.

Sometimes at the dentist,
You have to sit still.
Your mouth's open wide so
The dentist can drill.
Then all of a sudden,
On top of your knee,
You feel something crawling.
Perhaps it's a flea!
'Don't move,' yells the dentist.
(You've started to twitch.)
But down on your leg,
There's a horrible itch.

Then sometimes in church,
When the sermon is long,
Your feet go to sleep,
When it's time for a song.

The organist plays
 with incredible flair,
But when they all stand,
You're still stuck in the chair!
'Wake up,' you say quietly,
But down on the floor,
Your two sleepy feet
Have just started to snore.

The worst of the snitches,
That seem to get me
Is when I am eating
Baked beans for my tea.
My taste buds are drooling,
Then deep in my throat,
A little wee bean
Makes me splutter and choke.
My eyeballs start rolling,
My face goes bright red,
Then somebody thumps me
In case I drop dead.

Those itches and snitches
Are not nice at all.
When you really don't want them,
They give you a call.
They come in the daytime,
And even at night.
They wiggle and tickle,
And sometimes they bite.
So watch for these snitches,
Whatever you do,
When they're tired of me, well . . .
They might just get you.

Grown-ups can be very strange

—Peggy Dunstan

63

All butterflies are beautiful
like coloured silks
that flutter.
I know they fly,
I see them
but why are they called 'Butter'?
And why are some all goggled at
and praised,
considered 'right'?
when everybody stamps and shouts
if butterflies are white?

I know they gobble greens and such
but then, I don't like cabbage much.

64

Flying home
—Elaine Lindsay

Towards sunset
they gather by the hundred
until the old elm
brims with birds
fluttering like leaves.
Such twitterings
you've never heard.

Then, strangely,
as if the leader called
'Get ready now,'
all is still . . .
Suddenly they're off!
Dark streamers
in the rosy sky.

Silicon chip
—Alan Trussell-Cullen

Did you hear about the dog
that swallowed a silicon chip
and became the world's first
digital watch dog?

65

Jennifer J.

—Peggy Dunstan

Jennifer J.
has gone to play
and left her room
in a shocking way—
the bed unmade
and her books upset
both socks muddy
and both shoes wet.
Father calls her
and Mother sighs
but Jennifer's gone
where the wild hawk flies
dancing away
the green hills over
sun on her face
and her feet in clover.

66

High rise

—Peggy Dunstan

The buildings
that are going up
reach
almost
to the sky
it nearly
breaks
your neck
to look
when you
are passing by.
And
shooting upwards
in the lift
I
nearly always
find
though most of me
arrives
intact
my stomach
stays behind.
It's disconcerting
with so many
all
about
the town.
I'm dizzy looking up
at them
and dizzy
looking down.

Mary, Mary, quite contrary

—Shelwyn Lee

Mary, Mary, quite contrary,
acts a little crazy.
She talks to flowers
for hours and hours,
and wishes she was a daisy.

68

69

The big, black whale
—James K. Baxter

I wish I were a big, black whale
Out in the deep, green sea.
He blows like a hose
Through the top of his nose
As happy as a whale can be.
And the sailors look pale
When they hear his tail
Go smack, smack, smack,
On a big wave's back
Out in the deep green sea.

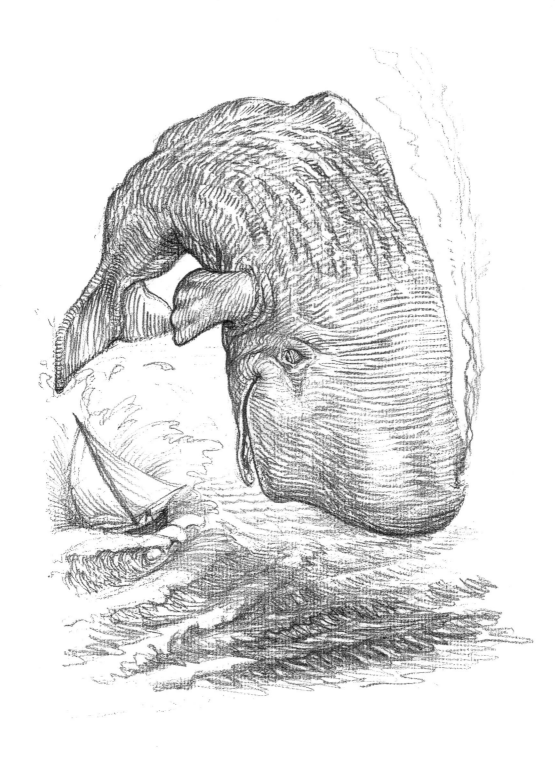

Pull yourself together
—Ruth Corrin

70

Can your ear touch your elbow?
Can your tongue touch your nose?
Can your fingers touch your feet and
tickle all your toes?

Can your mouth reach your ankle?
Can your forehead reach your knees?
Can your arms reach round your middle
to give you a big squeeze?

Can your fist fit in your armpit?
Can your feet fit in your lap?
Can your two hands fit together and go
clap, clap, clap?

Can your toenail meet your thumbnail?
Can your ankle meet your wrist?
Can your lips meet one another and have
a slurpy kiss?

Can your knee find your nostril?
Can your shoulder find your cheek?
Can your eyes find your eyelids and put
themselves to sleep?

The old owl
—James K. Baxter

'Tu whit! Tu Whoo!'
The old owl said—
'Pack up your toys
And get ready for bed.'

'As I sit on the branch
Of a grey gum tree
There's nobody here
But the moon and me;

'There's nobody here
But me and the moon,
And I'll go a-hunting
For my supper soon.

'A beetle, a bug
And a brown field mouse,
I'll bring them home
To my gum tree house.

'I'm old as old
And wise as wise,
And I see in the dark
With my great round eyes

'So hurry and scurry,'
The old owl said—
'Pack up your toys
And get ready for bed.'

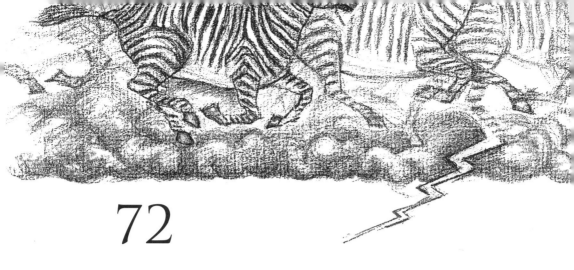

72

Who's afraid of thunderstorms
—Marlene Bennetts

Above,
thunder sounds—
hundreds of zebras running an African plain—
and lightning flashes brighten my room.
On, off, on, off,
as if someone is
flicking the light switch.
The wind moans and
slashes the rain against the window glass.
I'm not afraid,
I'll keep my head
under the blankets
until the storm goes away.

The windy night

(a poem for two voices)
—Vivienne Joseph

'Who's that
tap-tapping
at my window?

       'It is I, the flax,
       you hear
       a-tapping.

'Are those claws
I hear—
or bony paws?

       'Just branches,
       child,
       twigs and leaves.

'And that sigh—
so like a moan
and cold as dawn.

       'It is the wind's voice
       calling
       to the moon.

'Who licks
its teeth, one by one,
with a red, red tongue?

       'Why, Grandma's
       moonlight cat
       does that.

'Whose eyes so bright
chip diamonds
from the night?

       'The stars
       that's all, my child,
       and Grandma's cat.

'Who's there?'
I whisper.
'Who's there?'

       'We are here,
       so sleep now,
       sleep.'

Spelling
—April Wood

I spell well
always have.

letters fit nicely together
like magnets
slotting into position

I spell will
nearly always

sometimes letters shift
obstinately mischievous

I spill well
—I think

letters twist out of meaning
does that look right?
playing tricks.

I spill will?

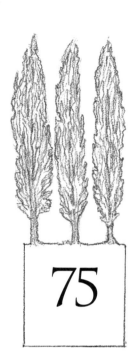

The poplars
—Elizabeth Spencer

Evening
and there
against the hurrying sky
the poplars stood.
Green candle flames
moving in the wind.

Their light
so filled my mind
I did not see night
sneak up from behind.

76

Ruru
—Marion Rego

All through the day, while the birds fly free,
Ruru sleeps in the old pine tree.
Deep in a hollow she hunches low,
And blinks her eyes at the sunshine glow.

When the sun goes down, and the shadows creep,
And the other birds look for a place to sleep,
Ruru stretches and looks around,
Her ears alert for the tiniest sound,
The wind has died, and no bird sings,
As Ruru glides on silent wings.

And now as the bush grows still and dark,
Huhu comes from under the bark,
Crawls through the leaves with a crackling sound
And his wings whirr shrill as he leaves the ground.

Ruru reaches with strong clawed feet,
And silently . . . silently . . . starts to eat.

77 The beach

—Tho En (Tho wrote this poem on her
Perkins Brailler when she was ten.)

I went to the beach one day,
As I approached,
I heard the waves roaring.

I felt the sand between my toes,
All warm and soft as a feather bed.

I heard the seagulls squawking,
Fighting for crumbs of food
Left behind after beach-goers had gone.

As the evening drew near, the warm,
soft sand
Grew cold and wet between my toes.

Who own the boats?

—Beth Braddock

78

During the week
while the people are away
seagulls own the boats
that are anchored in the bay.

But in the weekends
the seagulls must fly
to cliff-tops and watch
their boats sailing by.

79 Leaf play
—Stuart Payne

A leaf came up our path today;
it skipped, then paused upon its way;
cautious,
nervous,
suddenly it stopped—
right on the corner
down it flopped.

Upon our path the brown leaf lay,
quite worn out by its breezy play;
then slowly,
carefully,
up it popped and around the corner
the brown leaf hopped.

The fantail requests

—Bernard Gadd

80

'How can I catch,'
says the wig-wag
zig-zag fantail,
'juicy fat gnats
when your great
head's in the way?
Remember I share,'
chirps the flip-flop
zip-zap fantail,
'with you this air.
So please be fair,'
pipes the flit-flot,
rill-roll fantail.
'and leave me a little
bit of space.'

81

Moa
—Jon Gadsby

The moa was not the brightest bird
And couldn't fly, which sounds absurd
So wingless, this condition led
The moa to grow huge legs instead

But evolution must have frowned
On birds with both feet on the ground
For no one told him that those feet
Were not designed for bogs and peat

So when in fright the moa would stomp
Off recklessly into some swamp
Without the simple common sense
To figure out the consequence

Disaster came faster
The moa got slower
The mire rose higher
The moa sank lower

He thought he'd be like goose or duck
But moas are moas—and moas get stuck
While time and tide marched undelayed
The moa was stuck—and stuck he stayed.

He'd never really thought you know
And that's why he got caught you know
He hadn't even thought you see
And that's why he's extinct you see.

The silly song

—Margaret Mahy

Hey ding a ding,
    Hey ding a dong,
    Life is so silly
    and so is this song.
A telegraph pole is immensely absurd.
It stands on one leg like a sort of a bird.
It stands on one leg and pretends it's not there,
While workers on ladders are plaiting its hair.
    Hey ding a ding,
    Hey ding a dong,
    Life is so silly,
    And so is this song.

82

Wings

—Peter Bland

83

In summer
  grass, petals, twigs
  (the tips of things)
    quiver with a ceaseless
    insect shimmering

everywhere
there's a murmur of wings
a moth-blur
a gauzy quickening . . .
The entire landscape
is trying to take off!

84

The buffalo
—Jon Gadsby

The buffalo is big and black
It's really quite a pity
If he were small and pink instead
He'd really look quite pretty

The buffalo's inquisitive
Although he looks so dozy
But when you've got a nose like his
It's hard not to be nosy

The buffalo looks big and fierce
With horns upon his head
I wonder if he takes them off
Before he goes to bed

With horns like that it's difficult
The buffalo admits

To buy a proper sunhat
'Cause he can't find one that fits

And so he rolls in mud instead
And wallows in his pool
He ends up looking grubby but
I suppose it keeps him cool

The baby buffalo is small
He wanders by the side
D'you think they ever lift him up
And take him for a ride?

I think they should, considering
The trouble someone's gone to
'Cos all the buff'lo mums and dads
Have handles to hold onto.

85 | Australian rules

—Rae A. Williams

We told our Kiwi cousins
Don't forget your shoes
You can't run barefoot here
Don't step on twigs
Lying in your path
They bite
Don't disturb a burrow
All eggshells and old skins
Don't poke in dark shed corners
Or at a hollow tree.

Do remember
To hose out morning gumboots
Check the axles of your car
On a country drive
Be wide awake
To sleepy coils, unwinding
Stand well back
Lift your suitcase lids
With sticks
We told out Kiwi cousins—

Couldn't understand
Why they left
So soon . . .

In the library

—Howard Small

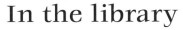

In the library
I can hear
Whispering of the books
Rustling of the leaves
Hushed mumblings of kids.
The sounds of silence are deafening.

When the library's empty
All the words come to life
Books open
Millions of words are released
Talking and chatting for hours
Then slowly but surely
They begin to return
To their shelves
And wait patiently
Always waiting . . .
waiting . . .
Until the library's empty.

87

Hark, hark, the shark
—Denis Glover

The professor, who is fond of fish,
Expresses as his earnest wish
That people shouldn't play the fool
With sharks about but stay quite cool.

If sharks are nosing round your beach
Just put yourself beyond their reach,
And when they're one or two a penny
Use your legs and arms, if any.

Don't thresh about, attracting more,
But quietly get yourself ashore.

Don't panic if you see a shark:
Its bite is much worse than its bark.

Bo-Peep's sheep

—Shelwyn Lee

The farmer's docking Bo-Peep's sheep,
that's why she couldn't find them.
She'll get a shock
because her flock,
now have no tails behind them!

Animal
—Jon Gadsby

89

Animal show us
Animal please
Animal show us as animal see
Animal teach us
Animal do
Lest we forget that we're animals too.

90

Wildlife
—Alan Bagnall

Is your house
A wonderful, huge
Wildlife refuge?
The odd mouse,
Two or three cats,
Ants under the mats,
Cheeping live proof
Of birds in the roof,
Geckos in the ceilings,
And a family or two
Of wild human beings?

The fantail

—Margaret Mahy

Green on the hill tops, green in the trees,
Green and silver in the wild bright seas.
But Jane found a place where the sun shone yellow.
Here danced a sharp little black and tan fellow,
Who twinked and who prinked on the bough.

Patchwork patterns on the dark leaf-mould,
Nets of shadow held the sun's hot gold
And he called to the world to be glad, to rejoice,
In a wheelbarrow-squeaking-in-the-garden-voice,
As he this-wayed and that-wayed,
He twinked and he prinked in the bough.

Oh, what a dancer! Oh, what a day!
('Boom' went the breakers in the wet brown bay).
And he danced in a fashion you were glad to see
In a crazy zigzag on a deep green tree.
As he
    High-footed—low-footed,
    this-wayed and that-wayed,
    he twinked and he prinked
On the bough.

92

There's a solemn wind tonight
—Katherine Mansfield

There is a solemn wind tonight
That sings of solemn rain;
The trees that have been quiet so long
Flutter and start again.

The slender trees, the heavy trees,
The fruit trees laden and proud,
Lift up their branches to the wind
That cries to them so loud.

The little bushes and the plants
Bow to the solemn sound
And every tiniest blade of grass
Shakes on the quiet ground.

93

I'm just pretending
—Peggy Dunstan

Stars are made of lemonade
The moon is made of honey
but no one's ever tasted them
which seems a little funny.
Except
    that they are far away,
so very, very high
and no one's made a ladder yet
that reaches to the sky.

The magpies

—Denis Glover

94

When Tom and Elizabeth took the farm
The bracken made their bed,
And *Quardle oodle ardle wardle doodle*
The magpies said.

Tom's hands were strong to the plough
Elizabeth's lips were red,
And *Quardle oodle ardle wardle doodle*
The magpies said.

Year in year out they worked
While the pines grew overhead,
And *Quardle oodle ardle wardle doodle*
The magpies said.

Elizabeth is dead now (it's years ago);
Old Tom went light in the head;
And *Quardle oodle ardle wardle doodle*
The magpies said.

The farm's still there. Mortgage corporations
Couldn't give it away.
And *Quardle oodle ardle wardle doodle*
The magpies say.

95

Josephine Jessica Julie O'Shea
—Joy Watson

Josephine Jessica Julie O'Shea
Lived with her Granny down Wellington way,
In a huge haunted house with a creaky front door,
With bats in the ceiling, and cracks in the floor.

Josephine Jessica Julie O'Shea
Rode into school on a broomstick each day.
She wore a black cloak and a high pointed hat,
And under her desk crouched a creepy black cat.

When Josephine Jessica Julie O'Shea
Invited us round to her Granny's to play,
We would feed her pet mice, and spiders and frogs,
And then collect cockroaches out of old logs.

Once, Josephine Jessica Julie O'Shea
Cooked a concoction all gooey and grey;
She sang as she stirred, and she stirred as she sang . . .
Then the whole lot blew up with a terrible BANG!

Well, Josephine Jessica Julie O'Shea
Mounted her broomstick and rode off that day.
With her cat behind her, and Granny on too,
She gave us a wave as she swept out of view!

The shepherd
—James K. Baxter

96

Where rivers tumble
In gorges deep,
High on the mountain
I muster sheep—

The scraggy, wild ewe
Who has never been shorn
And the big, rough ram
With his curly horns.

The sun shines down
Like a burning-glass
As they nibble the fresh, green
Tussock grass.

The tracks they make
With their nimble toes
No one but me
And my old dog knows.

With a long, low whistle
I send him out.
He cocks his ears
To hear me shout.

He is tired and dusty
Before the night—
His tongue hangs dripping
And his teeth gleam white.

When the cold stars glitter
And my door is shut,
We sit by the fire
In our mountain hut.

Snails are pretty sensible

—Peggy Dunstan

97

Beyond
my window
still
the night
is showing
just
a little
light
and somewhere
not far off
this bird
is soft-soaping
with coaxing word
a little snail,
in
accents sweet
and with
a most
beguiling 'Tweet'
assures
the snail
he wishes well
then
taps
and taps
upon the shell.
but
safe inside
it's quite all right
THIS snail
will not
be out TONIGHT.

The frog

—anon

What a wonderful bird the frog are—
When he stand, he sit almost;
When he hop, he fly almost.
He ain't got no sense hardly;
He ain't got no tail hardly either.
When he sit, he sit on what he ain't got almost.

98

99

Wellington's big, black umbrellas
—Bob Laws

In Wellington, you need
a big black umbrella
with an extended handle
braced to your chest
and strapped to an ankle.
The sides should drape
to the ground
with a slit to look out
so that you can proceed
with the wind, dry
—big black umbrellas, whistling by.

Do not drink strange things

—Anna Beeson (10) of Mellons Bay School.

Richard, Janet, Lisa and Drew
found in a paddock a witches' brew

They stirred it with glee till it was brown as logs
took a sip and now they're frogs.

100